WHILE YOU WERE APPROACHING
THE SPECTACLE BUT BEFORE
YOU WERE TRANSFORMED BY IT

WHILE YOU WERE APPROACHING THE SPECTACLE BUT BEFORE YOU WERE TRANSFORMED BY IT

LYTTON SMITH

NIGHTBOAT BOOKS / CALLICOON, NEW YORK

Cover image: *Due East over Shadequarter Mountain*
Matthew Rangel, 2007, lithograph.
Image used with kind permission of the artist.

Cover design by HR Hegnauer
Typesetting by Upstate/Maidavale

Cataloging-in-publication data is available
from the Library of Congress

Distributed by the University Press of New England
One Court Street
Lebanon, NH 03766
www.upne.com

Nightboat Books
Callicoon, New York
www.nightboat.org

And since I had the wit to understand
The terms of Native or of forreign land;
I have had strong and oft desires to tread
Some of those voyages which I have read.
Yet still so fruitless have my wishes prov'd,
That from my Countreys smoke I never mov'd:
Nor ever had the fortune (though design'd)
To satisfie the wandrings of my mind.
Therefore at last I did with some content,
Beguile my self in time, which others spent;
Whose art to Provinces small lines allots,
And represents large Kingdomes but in spots.
Thus by *Ortelius* and *Mercators* aid
Through most of the discover'd world I strai'd.
I could with ease double the *Southern Cape*,
And in my passage *Affricks* wonders take:
Then with a speed proportion'd to the Scale
Northward again, as high as *Zemla* sayl.
Oft hath the travel of my eye outrun
(Though I sat still) the journey of the Sun.

—Bishop Henry King

Error gathering. Listen with your eyes because here you cannot decipher what is said out of the effort of mouths.

—Myung Mi Kim

While You Were Approaching the Spectacle

Travel Narrative / 3

Of the Kingdom Which Counterweights Civilization / 4

Friendship as a Rhetoric of Retreating Past Borders / 5

Begins the Civil War / 7

A Turned Page as the Measure of Suspense / 8

By means of a mountain path or a merchant new-arrived
    or a fragmented map in a pawnbroker's: news travels, tells
    of a country through which goods might be easily moved / 9

International Natural Resources / 10

First of the Invasions / 11

Encounter with Elephants / 12

The Spectacle (I) / 13

Some Corner of a Foreign Field / 14

Trade Winds, Trade Routes / 15

Civil War / 16

Summer in the Delta / 17

Refraction / 18

Civil War (Forgotten) / 23

Native Characteristics Approved / 24

Bringing Violins, Games, and Bibles to Coastal Areas / 25

The Spectacle (II) / 27

River Insurgence / 28

Barefoot Across the Floor of the Pagoda / 29

'If' by Rudyard Kipling / 30

Independence Day / 32

General H— Flees the Abode of Kings / 33

Patriotism Does Not Doubt For National Joy / 34

Civil War / 35

The Spectacle (III) / 36

Moonlight at the Pagoda / 37

The Spectacle (IV) / 38

But Before You Were Transformed By It

Silk First Reaches the City's Markets / 39

Sweet and Fitting / 40

Telescopic Philanthropy / 45

Public Sites Are For Gatherings (Of Less Than Five) / 51

House Arrest / 52

Refugee Blues / 53

In the International News Headlines / 57

Civil War as the Longest Uninterrupted in World History
    (Forgotten) / 58

Monsoon Deluge / 59

As [They] Lay Dying / 60

On Empathy / 62

The Spectacle (V) / 64

International Disaster Relief Fund / 65

Civil War / 66

Resettling the Capital City / 67

The Spectacle (VI) / 71

As the Teak Forests Move / 72

We Are Here To Protect Even By Necessary Imposition / 73

Where Were You in This? / 74

By means of a military state and the governmental control
    of goods, carbon resources, travel visas, food, and labour;
    in the wake of historical occupations by and upon the national
    construct; through the resituation of villagers, villages, and
    language; offering momentary promises of alternative behavior;
    because it would be wrong to tell authority that its policies
    have failed; hamstrung by sanctions (except those related to
    global concerns such as rare wood, oil, pipelines, etc); dismayed
    by the mis-perception of people-minded rule, we have reached
    this stage of national happiness: / 75

Colour

detached

]Grafts[

You are coming to save us,
aren't you? The question is
whether to attempt to recover
an original that is at best in a fragmentary state.
So, if you want me to weep
first show me your own eye
full of tears; the fearsome
and the piteous may arise from
the spectacle.

                Something is wrong
with this picture. The object is
to fob us off with some kind
of portable anguish—that's to say
anguish that can be from its cause,
transferred in toto and lent to
some other cause. All that is left
now is to prepare an obituary
for the population.

The Airwoman Observed

You, barefoot, wonder. You barefoot wonder. You trans-
versal, you queen arriving from opened-up blue skies you
define horizon as where we disappear. Here you are

dusty earth and kicking off your shoes like you don't give
a damn, like the pagoda's marble floor could tether you
for now, for good, as if the shoes you left waiting

at the foot of the steps three hundred feet below, back
where the imperial masters told you what you should
and shouldn't do—how high and far they'd let you go

and what to wear—were the last weight you had to cast.
You sudden visitor, you no ordinary tourist, you set them
straight in your own queer way. You spent all your dolor

getting here and now you're all the joy a girl can be,
your step as barefoot as local custom. You're as much
a boy as any of these bent monks. You've set your eyes

on their terracotta robes. They look like desert approaching.

Satellite Image at 96°37'7.72"E 22°3'10.16"N

Loam roads pink with clay
seen bird's-eye-view through
spores of dark green treetops
beside logged and cleared plains.

An apparent stadium, a pool
with Olympic proportions,
metonymic for international
observers, world participation.

Or cooling tanks adjacent river
fissures necessary for reducing
the temperatures of fission/fusion,
at a remove from the cities.

Munitions factory, power plant,
standard military complex,
unanticipated military building,
spectacle as speculative site.

Your satellite entry within
the borders of the country
in question. This far-reaching
sequence of connected events.

Scale Model (Prism, Tamped Earth, Water)

In the calm behind the carnival, it begins.
metonymic for what exactly
We try to formulate a description for those who'll later ask,
and a catch with mirrors
try to go beyond a simile that contains it
as our hands contained   flexible geometry,
rising tides, windhovered water
multiple-sided   the tympanum
or the colour our eyes aligned
with   ignited civil unrest   cross and disperse
protest suppression   a suspense in orange,
the wet peat scent burred to our skin days after.

Behind the carnival   the transportable climate
at the fraying limit of celebration
the calm tremors and is not calm.
mechanized catch, and disperse,
cross. Set gestures.
There is no name for this,
no linear narrative.
We set the sand in motion
cannot hourglass the revolution

from experience to the telling
of experienced, demarcating and ordering
sound striking the tympanum
dyes in the set gestures of sense, inscription
transportable   a fired climate,
protest tides, civil
fluvial suppression

Our tales cross and disperse. In any climate
             music and   light. mechanized
             fired earth   and a catch with mirrors.
                     Mechanized light
                             calm reproducible mirrors
                                              try the set gestures
             in any climate metonymic   geometry, flexible, music

             transportable for what exactly
                                              report absence

It Took Place in a Town I Think Called M—

It would have been what people came for, if they came: a red
etched onto the central lake; the local official's son serenading
what exactly on the far bank. "I have needed you for leaving you,"
he seems to say, "the shadow the monastery casts doesn't elsewhere,

I won't forget you anywhere." They would have come for evenings
giving way—curtaining—to night, lamps building into a sky.
Someone's daughter hanging off a balcony like a trapeze waiting
for motion, for clockwork. Would have been the voices of

her parents friends and lovers come for. Voices, and ropeladders
trellising the hilltop pagodas, where the monks are visible
and invisible as the spectacle. "How did you travel?" the people
ask. "Well," you reply. And settle to local colour, the aniseed

of liquor, sat at outside tables here where interiors are neglected
as the spectacle is. "Not so much to see as pause," you are told,
"not so much a destination as a site for passing resources through."
Would have been what people came for, the image at its halt

on the disc of an iris. The people bridging even before leaving
the synapse from sight to spoken, located in the act of telling
to the distance and direction of home the spectacle, its surfaces:
"It took place in a town I think called M—, or would have

Your Event Horizon

We miss, sometimes, the normal, natural phenomena,
  the approach road running aground in a clearing.
  Someone says the lights are out, above and past

  as light is. We've battened our homes to land,
given the domestic up to ballast. A car arrives, another,
  a wilderness of cyclists, slowly the pedestrians.
  Scanning the distance for the incoming event:

  a wave cresting too high for its fetch, rolling tidal
to this headland. The sulphured illumination of firework
  writing the sky. Recovered twilight. A glacial tremor,
  unrest shuddering / the visible sign the interior's

  shifted / the headland, then the tumult of debris.
Evening ending unchanged: the lift of bay wind, the fade
  of bay wind, our conversations whispering out.
  Our watches set to local time, to depart.

Your Physics Experiment

AIM / PLAN

To trust or cover, as in to awning and entrance. Experience suggests the person later entering the room—you [...] welcome—visualizes its colour as a different hue. Somewhere mechanic your lower order brain has repurposed vintage devices; your retinal afterimage detaches itself. Observation equals what happens when you look away, a sign of fixstitch in the works or a gremlin in the photorespondent machine. Investments in saturation terminate in invisible fracture. What at the end it manufacts.

METHODOLOGY / REQUIRED EQUIPMENT

Torn. Tuned. Picked foxgloves, recycled into a tincture by which the heart's action settles a globe turning us but seen from within, its traceable curvature, its dyed landmasses, its translucence. Leaving it to the earth itself, with curvature toward horizon. Applause signals you have seen enough, disperse. If at the end, what disaster could you aver? Your memory is a colour memory, redstriped, whitestriped, unrolling, staging a site. If at the edge, a traceable faultline—involved.

HYPOTHESIZED RESULTS

A plausible circuit links serially the disparate events in an outcome. Erasure habits one response but premised on the on/off before/after model: telescope as opposed to electric current. This threshold of without movement yet present in the open field of air space. This collapse now here where the charge is a word-curtain live behind which images which image of remains. Remembrances of the blurred distant, what a tragedy is the adventure from the documentary into the empathetic. Safe, now.

GOVERNMENT RECOMMENDATION ON SUBSEQUENT MODIFICATION

Would've wished a lyric subjectivity, not a science lesson. Would've lessened nothing and injected emotion into canvas. A consensus is towards feelings as a way to awning and entrance, and not experience. The person later entering the room—you—has no obligation to colour.

Your Light Experience

The warmth you
are meant from what you create: a spectrum,
a rainbow laid out on the limited rectangle
of a page. Colour did not exist for you and does,
blurred at the edges. The sound of an emergency,
voices passing the open window, and you are
no longer sure what light is as it surrounds you.

Your Strange Certainty Still Kept

Here we have been long enough

to miss the other laws of nature:
water falling according to gravity
the weeks between sunset and rise
a word sounded and not excised.

Today, no body in the streets
and nothing visible of massacre
like shells cobbling the market,
the purple of blood in the road

but the university sealed until
notice, the monasteries bell-silent.
This present is the management
of bodies, their forcible movement

from a communal place to another.
The wet thwack of labour carries
from the ricefields and a fishboat
struggles the river. In teahouses

no one will talk of government
silence is a necessary wisdom.
The prison centering the city
a sight visitors do not visit.

The light here is most beautiful.

The News from M—

Here, where you all are,
language is an accessory

to bodies lying in the street,
prone in government rooms,

bloated in the waterways.
Or language is an accessory

to the refutation of bodies
lying etc. This too will pass

as search vessels in the delta
pass for smuggling operations

bringing illicit food to refugees
being autocued for media

appearances. What commerce
would you with us all. What

coverage can you offer for
coastal breach, aid refusal,

for the taut sinews and caught
breath of seated uprisen monks.

The Spectacle

I

The remote. There, in the Pavillion, the world,
a grotto, cornet-shaped, its shell closed from the viewer,
much a cave, an aggregate of the isolated. The image

observes the form of a fishing boat entirely,

its relations to the whole of totality

as if, from one point, all sides of the world
illustrate the same perspective: the eye's orientation is collapse.
Fissures in our gaze. Rest, laughter, overlooking.

                    This control of the situation—
of seeing—has a schematic. Thousands
are present, are repetitions of distance, a meeting

of the body and its situation in the world. The ordinary

codes of our surroundings harbour the moment we
experience the spectacle. Both a vision and

the world seen. Both looking and participating.

Your Projected Horizon

Event gathers in the corner of your eye:
a sandaled foot disappearing down an alley
as a door's sunk hinges swing a torso out
into the process of eyes downcast under
broad-brimmed bamboo hats, trained away
from, say, a crack that trails the part-tiled
roof of the teashop to an estuary where sky
collaborates in watching, suspends a glider's
aerial imagination of what routes and habits
people tread into local history, the rest of the body
the ankle belongs to, the suspicion whispered
in the instance before silence means the teashop
is no longer safe for speech, sandbags shutter out
images of rising water, the repetitive event gathers
in the corner of your eye, light brought to a focus
on receptors for colour, not detail, for blur.

New International Standard

In one version of the rules the commentators
will be lost for words won't find them
as the roof slides under the sky closing us
from the elements. We see we tied our safety
to colours and sometimes the most beautiful
phrase in a language is an expression of belief.
There are decisions I don't follow, reactions
the body has within its range and lets steal out,
a way of forming and deviating from assigned
patterns that takes my breath elsewhere. After
water next in the sequence comes community,
and it is riots equally as it is salvage. The feats
the body manages are athletic even at the stillest.
In one version of the rules the game continues
so we never have to answer the questions
of eventuality. A wave is tiding the stadium.
The goal line will extend around the world
even if I don't feel you, distant, crossing it
or get to break the plane beside you. Even if
the crossing of a boundary is not a resolution
it has a sound that cannot be octaved. Inside
a body inside a stadium. Lost for words
and elements I think of how a contest asks
of us a form of belief: in the dome several
pitted together act a persistent opposition.
I have painted a line on the ground. Where
it coincides with the end zone, the heat
shimmers visibility. This the eye believes.

Conversation Within/External to the Spectacle

"All representations, especially those of this nature
in court, public spectacles, have been or ought to be
the mirror of man's life." "These shows are nothing
else but Light and Motion." "As I stood watching,
I looked over the heads of those beneath me, forgot
indeed they were, in a trance at the machinations."
"Like to a garden in its transience, eternally reliant
on some guiding but invisible hand." "The populace
is taken unawares by a trick with images thrown
between reflections unawares that takes the populous
into a prison of words. Insanity." "Meta-" "A trapdoor
for" "Behind you, where you are a performer and
the audience sees—not hears—a spectacular entrance."
"A small or large machine, assembled as if before
your eyes." "But afterwards, dust and the viscous
of cog-grease. A hand injured in the rigging." "By
mirror, do you mean reversal?" "A light emotion,
of less value than a nothingness." "An aspect of it
has us on guard: we stood watch, our heads, heads
of those beneath us, alert." "A maze of distractions
and misdirections: one sizeable vista of a battlefield
lifelike enough to suggest real bodies, to remind us
of the vital importance of simile, alike to a damsel   Somewhere, far off w
in a tower, grey-eyed." "Tricked, rigged, happening   we think of as the w
elsewhere and made to look apparent." "Reflections   as places under-deve
"The rhythms of speech used"ready for the showing, huge scenery is being
"Colour thwarts our eye the relocated villagers are given presentation ratior
"Back to languagreminded people who tell all truth are happy, the generals
"Patter a path of bulrushes laid to staunch the mud. This photosensitive spec
This picture shows nothing wrong. Imprinted proof against an aesthethics o
lines moving us fallibly within the audible evidence of the location in quest

And after

you circumambulate the event horizon   refraction is
given the papers necessary for travel   eventual documentary
relative to the truth of the event (pl.)   in relation to what

For colour, after all, is errant.
Had thought
the orange saffron the monks wore,   terracotta
were not warriors but conduits   (maroon) in the next frame
photographic reprints of monks   the junta will
disappear   disappear

                        keep your eye on the patter

(the eye flickers imperceptibly, falters)
                        re-read the junta your eye just passed over
                        re-read the line your eye just passed on

parse the shutter of blink in terms:

is there a mathematics of worldview   of nervous skill.
                                                of approach &
circumspection:

Let spectacle equal the last event to alter your settlement.
        A pair of ducks emergent on a calm.
        The nonsequence of the book.
        The flooded plains also were flood plains.
        The monks still lying in the road after the bodies are taken.
        The monks still lying in the road after the bodies are taken.

                        keep your eye on the patter

Working with numbers you calculate the assumed toll percentage.
Backsolve for radical and radial. Discover misuses for equation, analogy.

Your Orange Afterimage Exposed

I tend to a romantics of colour

    the monks are in their orange
    and orange is this laughter
    of unison I can place as those

passing outside my apartment
languages abroad from where
their monasteries sit empty.

    I miss sometimes how a body
    is removed and goes unnoticed.
    What it takes in oxygen and sight

and gives in noise. There are those
who cannot speak of disappearance
and those for whom it means nothing.

    Sheltered here I write places I
    am not, as if the work of sound
    echoes where touch and sight have

faded. The streets, the fields of M—
are peopled still and peopled also
with their absents. Orange is a word

I think for massacre, for untold.

Massacre

]Grafts[

All that needed recording was
the fact that a sort of geological
tremor had apparently taken place.
The phenomenon was duly noted,
dated, and deemed sufficiently well
understood; a very simple sign, "the
fall of the B— wall" repeated over
and over again, immediately attained
the incontestability of all the other
signs of democracy. I knew the place
already from the satellite imagery
and Google Earth, but being
here personally is a bit different.
Peizing each syllable of each word
by just proportion.

Destination to Ghost

A boy plays a cassette recorder's
graveled voices & to whom do they
belong as the historic restored pier
eases into flame for the fourth time
in four decades. A measure of time
the end-of-the-line inn collapsing
through its wooden floor & into
the north sea. The oak bar adrift,
the kegs burning timber & ethanol,
the fairground dulling with soot.

If the owners of the voices unreeling
are the seasonal visitors whose coins
the boy finds in winter, their metal
& figurehead his want for elsewhere;
if the fire subsides; if the arcade's
neon & electric were to wash over
anything but the empty seafront
of a place on route from destination
to ghost. Light hesitates in the heat.
Horizon is a story told by strangers.

Tell Me About Your Miraculous Invention

In monochrome it
was reminiscent
of a silent film

a clash choreographed
between grey figures
and grey figures

leaving some dead
and some facing
the camera, restoring

to the town its
everyday hawking:
life persisting where

it isn't ended violently.
The movie theater
thick and noiseless

we have nowhere
to go but out where
the ordinary occupies us.

The Apparatus to be Useful

Independent observers in the central square
converge where events have the sad familiarity
of accordion music: the protesters as seated
as inert paving stones, the park gates sealed
as if by official order, gunfire opening
like an elevated firework. It's the manic
at the show who makes the crowd

panic. Before the discovery of perspective,
before vanishing point, I imagine—
but this is nostalgia, knowledge of
the lost, which is to say, invention.
The uprising is crushed and this time
we call it fair. The uprising is crushed
but living, here, is hard as well. There

are revolutions per minute, there
is the information super-highway.
We went along the stepped creek
yesterday, and a red woodpecker
insistent and hidden in the branches.
The internet can be switched off
and those outside describe the land

as gone dark. The fields have furrows
labourers, and crops. Evening beams
of log trucks and the military police.
Out in the silence we wait for them
to come back online, into light.
I see your beams, we write, but ours
have long teaked out. Tomorrow

will find us woodheaded, forage
and thought-full. In your corner
of the world, light is most beautiful.
There isn't, this time, a theatre to leave.
The remains remain in the central
square and then are vanished, the central
square renamed. Relocated: the central

square remains but on the map is south.
The audience decides what's spectacle
and how it ends. Light casts a region
in visible colour but we know it after-
effect, post-produced: an imperceptible
wave traveled and out-of-date activates
chemicals in the retina and we feel

sight: the idyllic agricultural scene
where an uncertain implement rests
beside the workers; perched gargoyles
on a temple; how humbled by light
we are; how wrong it would be to pass
this way without seeing: plains, receding;
a contested election; a travel brochure

ending its peripatetic route from land-
scape to captured image to printed
paper to half-thought of travel: a part
of the possible globe, revolving and
coming to a stop on its teak stand.
The wind chimes, the poplar trees,
a newspaper, ink-wet and thick-leaved.

II

The world is a room in yellow
where scale is a mode of the retina, sight
a possible experience. An exhibition's socializing
strategy, each element a navigation through the cross-field.

The museum has its own polemic. The machine
has gestures. The institution, its consumers;

the market, its activities. What transpires
is a confrontation with meticulous organization.

We wonderfully cross from the experiential foyer
to where light has a frequency. To orient the landscape

is one objective.

Feasibility Study (Scale Model Anticipation)

legality, sta

indelibly   legible   ineligible   what we are looking towards is:
     Led in by their chains not by their captors
     deliberately as in with reflection as in

     reflection: literal? The figures doubled by a surface, possibly fluid,
                 what we are looking towards
reappearance then at the left edge of the scene but not necessarily in a con
narrative fashion.

          from a purely geographical perspective
          the aesthetics are more promising than
          one would have imagined, don't you think?

in delight. I need little. Won't reiterate the iterated   gestures requir
but reitinerant, the light most beautiful
in all our terribleness / meet me at the tavern   cannot avoid e

What to do about a sense of scale? Acres, masses: the populous
people, peering, the public: those looking

                   seeing those looking
are looking towards us   a way to mandate the use of space in ritu
          back somewhere with the illusion
, the way travel is just one more magic trick   of progression—leav
               no, changing colou
       and here at the centre, as if a pivot
the center will not and etc   here we abut the edge of wha
midday sun, a foreign field   a responsibility to craft, to the
procession, regalia.   weighting each syllable accor
elements for a measured response   a measured response to the tr
(When I said "in seeing in one sees a different sight than seeing from an in
lately external" I meant not the inherent variety of viewpoints but the tran

hindsight a sequence of events progresses with a cartoon flipbook staccato. A figure in
racotta threads the crowds in the former capital's streets. A period demarcates the events
tween one punctuated terminus and a later time. The presence of authorities and spies

Mad Dogs and Englishmen Palinode

vents the vendors edging the streets from selling bootleg DVDs of the on-going natural
aster. Keep your eye on the terracotta cloth slipping through the loose consent of the
cessary residents. A spark of light, like early sun across the polished, almost glass surface
a small metal object, a razor, perhaps, or a spoon. The figure in terracotta carries no

In tropical climes there are certain times of day

s bowl. The main hotel is named for the famous hotel stranded in the imperial capital

When all the citizens retire,

y centering the regime which once seized this country. You have not been within the

to tear their clothes off and perspire.

undaries of these interconnected events long enough to parse them. Along the route a

It's one of those rules that the biggest fools obey,

phazard spiral of accidental tourists searches a route to the pagoda. Earlier, the streets

Because the sun is much too sultry and one must avoid

re vacant in order for the military to stretch its legs and divide the insurrectionists

its ultry-violet ray—

m the populous. The figure's dyed robes weave an opening of thin air through the

Papalaka-papalaka-papalaka-boo. (Repeat)

wds. Even without their olive-green skin, military agents must always be present and

Digariga-digariga-digariga-doo. (Repeat)

cognized. The figure disappears into the crowd which has all the kinesis of looking at

The natives grieve when the white men leave their huts,

mosaic. A traffic light remains paused red and a policeman dissuades a tourist from her

Because they're obviously, absolutely nuts—

nera. The passive voice should always be avoided in order to express the direct action
a sentence's agents. The figure resurfaces at the foot of the hill which bases the pagoda.

Mad dogs and Englishmen go out in the midday sun.

s head still, neck taut, he begins to ascend the steps for the final time. In two years' time,

The Japanese don't care to, the Chinese wouldn't dare to,

day's light rainfall will have been forgotten in part because of a storm of heavy daffodils.

Hindus and Argentines sleep firmly from twelve to one,

anslating a word into another reveals a catachresis—an abuse—in communication.

But Englishmen detest a siesta,

om a distance, the figure's serene progress up the steps offers a simile for the region's

In the Philippines there are lovely screens,

oblems. Barefoot, the figure reaches the three hundredth step where the airwoman

to protect you from the glare,

ood not far from oil drilled where he stands. A spark of light, early sun from a polished

In the Malay states there are hats like plates,

e onto the almost-glass surface of a metal instrument, a razor, perhaps, or a spoon. The

which the Britishers won't wear,

me of the central prison means a word for lunacy in the colonial language and in the

At twelve noon the natives swoon, and

y's language means a sentence is imposed arbitrarily when someone's actions fit the

no further work is done—

ohibited descriptive space. The figure circumambulates the pagoda's marbled floor,

But Mad Dogs and Englishmen go out in the midday sun.

cing pedestrian circles clockwise. Rumour: tunnels, rooms, treasure buried below the

It's such a surprise for the Eastern eyes to see,

goda. Since this is the most illustrious religious structure cameras circumobserve the

That though the British are effete,

racotta figure's circles with wide shutters. The area's problems reduced to a question

they're quite impervious to heat,

out what might be done to help from a distance. A spark of light, early sun from a

When the white man rides, every native hides in glee,

lished tile onto the almost glass surface of a razor drawn by the silent monk across a

Because the simple creatures hope he will

ised, taut neck. A sentence ensures the location and activities of those opposing the

impale his solar topee on a tree.

thors of, say, a constitution, a poem, a disaster response. In the official story, the monk

s prompted to suicide by financial problems. Rumours of tunnels, rooms, treasure

Bolyboly-bolyboly-bolyboly-bad. (Repeat)

low the pagoda unburied by the military junta. Midday sun, everyday hawking,

Habaninny-habaninny-habaninny-haa. (Repeat)

thing to report from the coastal sites, the city unstilled by the overturned alms bowl.

It seems such a shame that when the English claim the earth

Scale Model (Bodies, Dyed Fabric, Incendiary D

In the calm behind the carnival, it begins.
You will sit in the arterial road and pray
Internally, in the city center, the officials

in silence. Will wind through streets, will
write a column in which street protests
wait a reaction. The idea of end troubles

have gone out of fashion. At this writing, live
a rewriting, another installment in the serial
bullets have not been ordered. Disruptions

form. We are wiring the concerned global
in the internet occurring sporadically until
newspapers when it happens again. Time

the scenario is more presentable to foreign
travelling backforward this event was where
visitors. If you can't see the street for the monks

before and we felt nothing, watching, slow
then the mandala protects you with its colour,
threaded in anabranches that become the tsunami

an official suggests. Reading between the lines
building along the sounds of the coastline: sudden
is only possible if you're allowed lines to begin

disrespectful recurrent. We have been here
with language, access to communication,
before. Hand-sewn the garment and dyed

the order to sow bullets among the people,
with the shells of ironwood fruit, with ficus root,
the whole population in the streets, the whole

population is in the streets, achingly colourful.

Wish All Know the Truth

                        I've traveled here before
I think: a clutch of shaven-headed men

grouped serene, the nerved swelter
of dense summer air and death is itself

is noise and consequence, is invisible.
The streets in the afternoon after are

empty   the red steeping the pavement
a water-buffalo gunned down enraged

intruding on the town. I'd agree with you
what red is, where on the spectrum it

resists the path of light and rebounds hue
and meaning—and this is where we are

lost. You could manufacture red with prisms
and beams and call it warning. You could

dye the streets as if a hundred hundred lay
down in the semblance of a massacre

to be retrieved in an official language
denying colour its emotion and colour.

Those gathered men are still so distant.
Try this in monochrome and what results.

The News from M—

The city's dearer, continental
eateries are as familiar as you

would expect, given you were
here all along. Print rubbed

black off on your hands,
here's colours linger on

while your brain names terracotta
(maroon) saffron having seen ferrous,

hæmoglobin-rich red. Names it
M—. It tragic. It urgent. It

monk for sister, it sanction for
sanction. It the brain functions,

it the eye sure-sighted tells all
its truth and people are happy,

it is redevelopment restoring.

Ushahidi.com

look we have crowdsourced, here I am typing here is I typing this I saw wr
on the ground we are typing this we have put down in a text this I was wr
and uploaded the crowd is the source the crowd a solution of particles wri
what the crowd was saw in its dissolute in its dispersal and brought to our
attention is typing in ways that are horizontal and outgrowing so that the
testimony does not disappear beyond the edge of the page as its slides the
information down with the sediment of more information that we were wr

for the crowd forms from its sources
and sees what in the distance we hear
later sound traveling slower than light
to our eyes. In places the crossborder
technologies are stonewalled, ushahidi.
Ushahidi in the wake of the flood
ushahidi against the violence against
the dissenting exercising the electoral;
ushahidi the public domain or normal,

sudan vote monitor cui
voto chile crisis map th
gaza open forest italie
peace heroes Snowmag
Cleanup congo drc hai
map south africa wildl
kenya connection geom
atlanta crime error 40.
stop stockouts crowded

ushahidi in open source we are sometimes in languages other than
sometimes binary strings computing worldscripts and googleeyeview
ushahidi what happened all categories defamation voting access disturbance
campaigning what went well arrest candidate withdrawal removal of observ
todas las categorías alteran los resultados el acta o las boletas robo de urnas
incompleto ofrecen dinero a cambio del voto hacien campaña el día de la e
propaganda en la violacion del voto secreto fotografia de voto hay violenci
in a parenthesis (the elections will have to be re-run) event happens to tho
in translation approaching the spectacle remotely
you see the dovetail of a greenroof and cedar (teak?)
smoothed into dwelling you see what colour sites
in the memory by transmission, by flagged overlaid maps,
by word on the ground on the sapling pages of a guide
you kaw-wah-la, you outlander, you foreigner, you
implicated and witness, you unavoidable event.

Travel Writing

Or I have not been here before.
This movie theatre. This movie theater.
A revolution leads to sunset, the salmon

emboss of clouds against an evening.
The glass face of a corporate structure
edged beautifully with the reflection

of corporate structures. Here you are
not lost for things to do. The walk
to the famous monument takes you

past the inaccessible street musicians.
The city on the brink of sunset yet.
The walk you musician with footstep

ventures (it was folly to go barefoot
but you did) and inner compass.
There are side alleys but it is sunset

there too. The way a place is delimited
by colours you are too. Eagerly so: scents
along the avenue, imported skylines.

The lost gather at airports, silent
as geography. Observing their waiting
we expect flight   you   I   this theatre.

III

Wonder creates navigation. Granted, the spectacle
is counterweight to entrance, multiple as index.

The different registers of orientation compacted
for the purposes of variation.
                              Developed activity forms

spaces. Trains in motion emerge through risk

to meet with scenography. Simplicity is a stone
collided with ice and tiled, the pieces of a mosaic
unfolding interminably in the mirrors. A measure

of illogic to the infinite. Revolving is a pattern
woven in glass, changing as entrance. Stroboscopic

is the room's sole form. Character a simple
experience. The mind: familiar with reality.

The People's Glossary of M —

Teak: Houses unstructured for timber, home
          a concept. Logging trucks are our
          country renamed and headed exterior.
          What is natural about resources?

Parade: An indoor day. The cease to wayfare.
          In the bazaar, in the teahouses, words
          have their echoes. You are repeated. Dawn
          you may be ceased. A performance of force.

Visitor: One who travels assigned roads unaware.
          One complicit but unaware. One contact
          with the outside world; a risked imprison.
          Communicate hurriedly. Pseudonymous.

History: As anyone's. In the tale handed down
          parent to child a youngster imagines
          beyond the village, travels the only road
          and hears each step a homeward wish.

Military: Too long now. Too long now. When
          you have learned from our struggles
          to voice, we will be here. Disappeared.
          Within the cage we have tried wingspan.

History: What you have written about. The tale
          of uprising, of a courageous and threatened
          member of the opposition, her house arrest.
          within—the cage we have tried—wingspan

IV

Tiles, direction, the whole movement is militarist:
hovering and taking possession of the situation.

Once Upon a Time in the Border Areas

your iris widening
into a lit interior

                      —the narrow of accustom—

of a foreign territory
where the massed saffron

robes are the history
of your childhood among

                     —pleasant is green temperate—

illustrated books, among
the saffron of suburbs

assembly is how you began
a schoolday, grouped hymnal

                     —a unison, an in chorus—

not the levelling of those
who gathered in maroon

silent or silenced
or written out of history

                     —or written out of history—

The News from M—

Think of the hollow of a bowl
as reception, a carved space for,

a promissory. Alms-space, social
as seeing across coastline. Upturn

that open hollow to roof, to seal
against gifting. To bar the soldiers

from a receptacle for their alms
is to ask for the prisoners' release,

the refugees' return. A hollow seal
against gifting as if holding out hands

not for aid but for a transformation
in what we might exchange. Leaving

free the space hollowed in the bowls
the monks carried upturned over

their heads: a penned-in tradition,
a handing over of space demanded

at arms' length. The civil war unends
even if there's no longer a tourist bus

for taking potshots at the insurgents
reclaiming their homes. All there is is

a space, social and hollowed in wood.

Interlude

]Grafts[

Insert: *vow of silence*

Camera Obscura

This matters the way light realizes the natural,
the constructed
                          angles on a building steadied
against the deforested ascent, descent

                          as if
the monastery placed by light represents
interim and in conversation with

                          as if
the candle lit is the presence of a deity

                          as if
when we abolish the symbols we lose
our situation we lose orientation.

                          You, you let yourself
                          be seduced

Clock. Font. The votives receive messages
at the threshold doorway to the sanctuary.

                    The fontwater disturbed
by a community passing into observance,
slight unease in the earth,

fingers dipped into water and touched to forehead.

        The clock loses time.

The clock is removed from the wall
and given time.

                    Before the bell
congregates the observers an observer
kneels in thought as dust sketches light
entering the monastery.
                              A passage from one
silence to another
                              and the acts of the body
—cord against the hands, tension and release
of the whole figure falling

                              and rising
marionette to sound, ear drum reverberating
stat crux dum volvitur orbis, not just
the globe but the world and its contents
revolving—

                    a translation into thought.

                              You, you let yourself
                              be seduced

one more sound among the sounds

                              the salt cellar
handled along the table, a wood spoon
knocked on a bowl, exterior weather.
                                     Silence
is a lesson language has to teach us: one
alone is not silent.
                        An observer working
a hacksaw across a felled tree trunk:
the sound of each observer unmistakably
her own.
                      An observer clearing snowfall
from the cropbed and sowing
                             colour.

And when it is necessary for an observer
to go through a town or village she
will be content to pass through only.

                    You, you let yourself
                    be seduced

And when it is necessary for an observer
to go through a town or village he
will be content to pass through

                              only

In admission we reserve the right to ask
that you leave.
                    In admission you retain
the right to depart.

                    Are you prepared to search
and observe what transcends the body?

                    You are novice.
In these surroundings you let yourself be
led aside, away.
                    You have watched
and have been watched, have been entered
into the building the way a sunbeam enters:

the image fades to silence and the eye
remembers the sunbeam: each recipient
thinking it theirs alone
                    like sound or colour
persisting after you have watched it pass.

Required Phrases (Your Sustainable Travel)

k'â-shin-dó â-thaìn-â-waìn-hma
beh-lo pyá-thâ-na-myò-dway-néh
yin-s'ain-nay-yá-dhâ-lèh?
                              sì-kàn-méh
k'â-yì-thwà-la-yày louq ngàn.
mi-di-ya t'eìn-c'ouq-hmú.
nain-ngan-yày mâ-ti-neyin hmú.
ba-dha-yày bâ-dí-beq k'á. Is travel
inland possible by bike? Or on foot,
the left of your rice harvest slung
on your back in a basket whose straps
mark the miles you've tried to intersperse
yourself into the jungle?
                              Language
terms this internal displacement, a shift
of people within designated borders.

Tell me again the problems of community.
So there is a necessity of your tourism.
k'àyi-dheh as one who leaves and stays left.

Events that take place don't take place
until you have seen and been transformed:
traversed formal borders, produced locally.

A View From Above, Beyond or After the Locati

Feet heavy and tender with the blood
hauled from the heart, tired hip flexors
tighten the legs to the inertia of gravity
—you traverse the internationally recog-
nised area of outstanding national beauty.
The breathtaking panoramic as the lungs
stage their laboured inflations/deflations.
The camera substitutes an image where
the eye retains a set of movable parts it
conflates over time. Piecework of recall.

Here you are at the coordinates given you
by a guide. You have unraveled directions
as though these rises and foliages in land-
scape—at the less reflective end of green
as a colour delimited by terracotta (a brown-
like red, oxidized hemoglobin) and maroon—
are themselves a description of a place
not the place itself. A citation. As if your story
here is projection, and in fact you nestle
neatly into an armchair's human tendency.

BEFORE YOU GO YOU SHOULD KNOW

avel to M— is not without its
fficulties or its ethical implications.
an your travelling well in advance so
u have time to secure the necessary
avel documents; visas have been de-
ed to tourists who have elsewhere
sited sites of disaster relief. Consider
hether this form of tourism meets the
eds of your adopted country: carbon
otprint, narrative vehicle, metonymic
ssibilities, analogical tenor, etc, etc.
here are people here on the ground here.

DEALINGS IN THE LOCAL CURRENCY

xchange rates vary unpredictably and
times those in the cities are aware
a devaluation in monetary symbols
ng before those in the countryside.
hat you spend might provide brief
d to those with curtailed employ-
ent opportunities or else further pad
e budgets of the government/junta
question. VISA will work worldwide.

GETTING WITHIN THE BORDERS OF M—

ntil recently, via a single six-seater
ane. Now six times daily via the near-
t country's national airline or else via
e charming bridge/border control
here a local guide attaches himself to
u in a manner of espionage or need.

INTERNET/E-MAIL/LONG DISTANCE CALLS

ccasional. There's a whole world
t there but the fictions of external
presentation (massacre, hunger) do
not mesh with the realities of the
juntament's M—. Your photographs
may be supplanted and/or doctored
and/or wholly excised from the record.

LITERATURE/CULTURE/ART/MUSIC/LIFE

Much has been written in this expansionist
language by the kala and kaw-wah-la
and their descendants, including a wist-
fully amusing account of how football
transformed the hopes and aspirations of
an entire country (the pages of this book
concluded before the privatization of local
teams and their assignment to the corp-
orate directors familiar to the juntament).

SIGHTS YOU MUST NOT AVOID MISSING

Despite frequent—some say continual
—occupation, M— suffers from a para-
doxical isolation breached only by the
most tenacious of natural/God-given
disasters and/or egregious of human
rights violations. Tourists should not miss
the spectacle, and are encouraged to ask
local informants or at juntament infor-
mation offices for the best and/or least
known methods of observing and docu-
menting the dramatics of the spectacle.

INTERNMENT

Lasts for renewable periods which are
specified but which bear an indirect re-
lationship to time as established by the
majority of calendars, almanacs, and Swiss-
crafted watches. Should you find yourself
within the lunatic prison, do not expect
rights, visitors, aid, family, release, light,

A History of the Present

]Grafts[

         The initial plan
was to simply map those incidents
to give to anyone interested a clear
picture of the situation on the ground.
Whatever the seer sees she must see
for herself alone—
there can be no other eye-witness.
The technology community has
set up interactive maps to help us
identify needs and target resources.
Electricity is a kind of wave, as are
my words, when they leave my mouth
as condensed air, spreading radiantly,
entering your ears:

See Things in Right Perspective and Feel the Truth

I watch the lights ending in the national bookstore.

Electricity's weak and brief, a tepid lime as it fades

in the afternoon. With lime the colonists whitewashed

hospitals and recovered from tennis. I'd tell you

people here are voracious readers and furtive

except here you're as like one of them as us

or else not here where the chance of conversation

is a luxury like satellite, cable, internet. What language

we're reading and speaking and how it names

the space from (t)here to horizon and over and over

isn't one we've chosen. Words are handed us

between pasteboard covers we teach our throats

to sound as glottal as the government wants.

The light ends in the national bookstore, like want.

Seeing Yourself Seeing

Take this small village. There's a crescent walkway
through marsh and irrigation you think opens
onto the sea where a tropical blue cottage
stands in the distance as if on the water itself.

The house is a trick of the horizon and the path
curves you away to the other small village.
You make your way east, assembling photographs
as proof. You have collected menus of restaurants.

There was a maritime store and an empty hotel
and you have taken them, your singular image
of the quiet edge of interior. You reach the other
village and here a store sells globes sealed around

rural buildings. White flakes note the foundations.
Someone thought this scene should have survived.

You Have Contravened a Mandate

Your modern espionage. A half a mile past
the line marked in the tide. A half a mile
marked by watchful intent. To have swum
in the world's ocean is nothing more than
to have settled the question whether one land
might lead to the next. You were following
from a distance the sky or a yarn, an element
lost in the telling: a name, the nautical speed
of a vessel approaching another vessel.
The sleight of hand by which you manage
your memories.

Application for Fellowship

The spectacle expects
to cha(lle)nge the visitor's
habituated movements
and orientation: patterns
in the neurological circus.

What if the spectacle
creates new patterns.
Tracking the green-
roofed barn, you see
the events of assembly.

The carpenter working,
his one functional arm
planes the trunks of Scottish-
Cherokee encounters into
the knot-holed finish
of a finished cabin.
Not the green of the roof
of the building seen but
what beyond its edges it
cites: an historical mountain

forest present for pages
and pages and pages and
pages of what are books.
The hike along a snowed
ridge where a steel tower
strays in the wind, observes

no fires. A satellite image with
a zoom and travel function. Earth
as dispersed as the dirt our treads
trail to the next destination.

Something to the left or right
of the edges of this picture.

The News from Poetry

Across the bridge, thread through
a   forest, and emerging
        find at the site of the
traces. We are   into radio
        unassembled, loose sinews
                participants   activity.
A history   moving image

moving us. Story of the moving
        moving on. Flickers
as of sequence   rrupted,
narra   , the   news suggesting
    are going   radio silence
the result   process
of distance   atlas, satellite,

censorwork,   acrostic
resistance and messages across
radio,   telep   wires, lines
    from the safehouse   metaphor.
    are going   to radio silence and
you   coming to   us, aren't you."
The last, most memorable, or most-

        cited   gravel voice;
    enduring photographic   ;
footage fatally   . We are
going into radio silent the telescopic
            working. Armed   urgence
        sanctioned   food has been
sanctioned   telescopic   ceased.

          alter as they magnify
We are   into   silence
at   of the spectacle a barn
as trans   looking wishes
          .   the carnival
at the fringes of   mourning
the loss of   daughter.

Evenings,   disembody of
        on a wireless device. Some
where   passes from
      to   and about   .
whereabouts the radio remains
We   into radio silence
where   a truculent

babble—like a brook—of voices
        , coming across a radio.
        , to safety, to the   –
mission   data   narratives
and non-   of   .
We   before;
      wrong with this picture. Noise.

V

        In various experiences of water,
the deal the viewer makes with the world
is the body in the employ of space. In place
of visiting: particles instilled via an aperture
into the interior. The Pavilion, a building in wood,
an aesthetic experience of art carved by light moving
in transverse to ourselves. (The spectator equally changes
the objects and influences of the person seeing.)
Oscillating structure and viewer, the situation of interaction,
the field and what it is called. Atuned to the sensory
and the cultural as when we (alone) turn to our fellows
and the world at bay, installed. We survive our surroundings.
Casting into the interior for the movement of images.
What actually appears casts light on our expectations.

Katamari Physics (Your Inventive Velocity)

The world is interspersed with sundries—
typewriter ribbon, signage, superhero,
schoolhouse, agriculture—and one body
attracts a smaller body. The sphere rolled
accumulates and your idea of the possible
expands. Anything of capital is in your reach.
The conquested mountain. Nth wonder.
Rain and its cloud foundations. This law
the world follows is rolled up in turn.

Your Position Surrounded and Your Surrounding

gone as a bridge is
crossed and past tense

or a possible hoped-for
crossed where the feat

of engineering is a faint
boundary failing eyesight

ear's reach you are etc
strung tension in the lines

where two or more lands are
ending together a history

of the present the colour
of the unfinished revolution saffron

plasma maroon red terracotta
what we saw was described

and in the description nothing
new but the number for whom

a bridge is a fictive
the future past all tense

Your Afterimage Legacy

Oceangrass & saltair, a herd
low moving. Not adherent
to the ruinfallen countryside

here a visible dismantling,
recourse to the newest dates.
Started again, rebuilt then.

Late summer, late dynasty,
not nomadic, not exactly.

Oceangrass & saltair, river
boat & ricefield, forest
alternatives: present cover,

covert home, nothing
ancient. Another body
to come, material worked

and worded to other forms.
Itinerant use, nomadic line.

Restless, quiet in jungle
canopies, the phut-putter
of rivered traffic removing

to new location the boards
of old homes. Removal
of raw resources—logged,

charted, pipelined—a new
infrastructure, an industry.

Oceangrass & saltair, home
imprinted in these places un-
familiar. Here the relatives

collide. The greenest of
robes. The loveliest of years.
Saffron. Your imagination

not nomadic, not exactly here.
Your historied presence, here.

VI

Bricks, the scent of fired earth, of tiles.
This experience of the physical: an instance
of lightning suspended across space. There

is static in the room. The raindrops a rhythm

the viewer can time and a lamp illuminates there
the atomized water: rainbow out of waterfall

felt on the skin. The work of colour is inside
the eye, alongside the world, until the world
resembles its phenomena. That play of senses

on what we have in common. From outside
you become a part of the exhibition. The room

rotates, by function, by motor. The way a light-

house captivates in movement. The way doubt
in the viewer is a sensitivity. You have entered
into a space of light- and colour-. The body

appears interior as we move, source and subject

of the surroundings we have hitherto met. We
sight possibility, the spectacle appearing open.

Scale Model (Cupped Hands, Conversation, Gat

Your hands a cool bowl of riverwater, a righted alms bowl

it begins

in the calm behind the carnival behind the retina, where the blindspot
                    or in riverwater
                    weeds, the oil and wear
                    of water traffic, the flesh
                    memory of the drowned, bloated and dissolved
                    in the sprung currents

or somewhere in a park the figurative necks of sunflowers
turning to watch the industrial sun collapsing what exactly
the municipal complining to dark as electricity fails again
          Your hands a cool bowl of riverwater, a righted alms bowl holding
          the uncensored lines from the teashop.

scorched earth in the ethnic	the commerce
independent state we raise our	vote, mandate
eyes but not our voices those	two weeks forced
words will see you arrested	voluntary labour

Your hands a cool bowl of riverwater, a righted alms bowl, a half-globe,
a reaching around an absence. Taking the form of holding,

          the content discontent and always a cipher
          the form uncensorable. Replace in the
          girlband's chart-topping song "Is this M—
          or is it the jungle" "I see you, you see me
          I'm gonna dance, because I'm free" the form
          of dissent remains your hands a cupped almsbowl
          of riverwater, fluent assembly of the dead and
          the oil of rivertrade and of more than five
          gathering in a square, determining a space.

Scenic

silhouette the leave-taking of the body

In your absence

captive in a window as a window gathers

will the quality of light to frail

density over time (theorem: the fluid existence of State)

light as all it takes to return

at the lowest gravity transparence hardens

the quality of intimacy, a crossing

into and over a crossing—membrane—change

and eventually impervious?

You have seen the described object
& the description was quite beautiful &
did not justice the object which was

as follows as the spectacle
the window stages

in silhouette, this/our, easiest of leave-taking

Addressing a Country as the Name You Like It

Mornings here people wake nomadic to find themselves resident
in the red glance of sunfall. Unsettled into the gap between state

and home. These are least errant roots. Trails etch far as allowed,
landmarks are more reliable than placenames placed here and gone—

(The redbrick silo lingers, a reedpipe for an underwater town.
Carved in the peepul trees, in the poplars, barkmaps for whom.)

One generation more people approach by duskherd and soyfield.
And after, by subdivision, almost sightless. Speaking a forgotten

language of place, using words as if distance is not. Towns
woodlands monasteries sloped retreats pattern out like dynamos

whirring fainter, fading in colour, closing at the edges the less we tell.
What we were advised about places we have not traveled flits

through the mind like settlers' roads, abandoned. If you follow,
what tragedy at the end could you avert. If at the end the spectacle

is a barnhouse greenroofed, horses unpaddocked? In this halflight
the idea of an end troubles me. Tell me how to know destination itself.

Where we'll find (y)ourself enclosed within the location in question.

Acknowledgments

These poems were sourced from government propaganda materials, art exhibition catalogues, radio broadcasts, national poetry anthologies, historical treatises, news reports, internet forums, and other archives.

Thanks to all at Nightboat Books for supporting this book. I'm honoured to be on their list, thankful for their care and attention. Special thanks to HR Hegnauer (especially for aviation) and most of all to Stephen Motika for his vision and his energy.

I'm grateful to the editors of the following magazines, who published some of this work and gave me the confidence to keep at it: *Catchup, Diagram, Ekleksographia, The Equalizer, Fawlt, Fiddleblack, From the Fishouse, Gulf Coast, Inside Fordham, Poets.org, Prospect, Tin House.*

I would not be here without the there created by Carey McHugh and Karen Russell; you gave me enthusiasm and exactitude in equal measure. This book began at Notchey Place, Tennessee; thank you to J.Carey, Nancy, and all (not least Chester) for warmth and hospitality, for giving me the space to write and think. The final poem is yours. 'The Airwoman Observed' is for and after Gabrielle Calvocoressi, whose jabs, feints, and rhythms led me on. At Lake Uttran, Joe North and Katja Lindskog gave these poems a vital hearing. Brent Hayes Edwards and the members of the Serial Poetics seminar at N.Y.U. wonderfully challenged my sense of a book's limits. Michael Golston did some much-needed neural rewiring. Warwick and Garth helped me find *Due East over Shadequarter Mountain* in June snow. I'm delighted to have Matthew Rangel's art as entrypoint; his are trails I want to follow. J. R. Fenn gave this book its first language, its vectors, its final shuffle. I trust her song.

This is for the people of M—, for those who live within the spectacle, if it can be.

NIGHTBOAT BOOKS

Nightboat Books, a nonprofit organization, seeks to develop audiences for writers whose work resists convention and transcends boundaries. We publish books rich with poignancy, intelligence, and risk. Please visit our website, www.nightboat.org, to learn about our titles and how you can support our future publications.

This book was made possible by a grant from The Fund for Poetry.

The following individuals have supported the publication of this book. We thank them for their generosity and commitment to the mission of Nightboat Books:

Kazim Ali
Elizabeth Motika
Benjamin Taylor

In addition, this book has been made possible, in part, by a grant from the New York State Council on the Arts Literature Program.

State of the Arts

NYSCA